BIKERS

BIKERS

HARLEY-DAVIDSON

People

This edition first published in 1995 by
The Promotional Reprint Company,
exclusively for Smith Books in Canada
and Chris Beckett in New Zealand

© Promotional Reprint
Company Ltd 1995

Designed by Blackjacks, London

ISBN 1 85648 313 4

Printed and bound in Malaysia

for Alastair and Alan

Introduction

Harley-Davidson motorcycles inspire a following like no other. There is a lifestyle associated with them. Events such as the Sturgis Rally and Daytona Cycle Week have become focal points for Harley enthusiasts.

Daytona is situated on the east coast of Florida, and the name has become synonymous with both car and motorcycle racing. The beginning of the year and, more recently, the month of March are the preserve of the two-wheeled community, with "Cycle Week" becoming an annual pilgrimage for not only American bikers but also for enthusiasts from all over the world.

The history of the event is longer than many may imagine. At the turn of the century the Ormond Hotel situated on Ormond Beach (adjacent to Daytona Beach) was a popular haunt of the wealthy. They travelled south by rail to take advantage of the warm weather at the beginning of the year. Two notable guests in 1902 were Ransom Olds, the founder of Oldsmobile, the giant American car firm, and Alexander Winton, another manufacturer of cars.

Legend has it that they raced up and down the two beaches, achieving speeds of up to 60 mph. Their activities sparked the hotel management into resurrecting a proposition for beach racing put to them in 1898.

The originator of the proposal, a William Morgan, was invited down to map out a beach race to be called the Ormond Beach Racing Tournament. The first one took place in February 1903 and was fittingly won by Winton.

In 1905 the first drag race took place on the beaches, and bikes started to feature in various racing activities. During the twenties and thirties, many record-breaking attempts took place, including one by Malcolm Campbell in Bluebird, who pushed the speed up to 276 mph on the sand.

As the speeds became too high for the narrow beaches, the record breakers headed off for the vast Bonneville salt flats in Utah leaving the "Birthplace of Speed" (as the area had become known) without an attraction to keep the visitors coming. The local authorities looked around for something to fill the void – and the hotels!

Enter long-distance motorcycle racing, which had been flourishing in neighbouring towns in the early thirties. In January 1937, the first running of the Daytona 200 took place – or to be more accurate, the "Handlebar Derby" as it was termed at the time. The entry set a new record, with 120 riders racing on a 3.2-mile course that was part road and part beach, connected by banked sand turns at either end.

The start area was at the south turn, with the best spectator area at the north turn, centrally placed in the middle of the town. All did not go well, though, as the organisers miscalculated the tide.

Starting at low tide the riders raced not only themselves but also the rapidly rising sea. The winner, Ed Kretz, averaged 73.34 mph on an Indian, and became the first to write his name on the City of Daytona Beach Trophy.

The next few years saw the racing flourish, and the spectators flocked back to the area when racing was taking place. However, the Second World War put an end to racing in 1942, until it was restarted in February 1947.

A record 184 riders took part in the sixth running of the event that took place on the same 3.2-mile course. Another record was the 27,000 fans who went to watch the riders battle for $1,000 first prize. This was to be the start of something big.

Newspapers at the time recount that the "city fathers" asked the townsfolk to open their homes to visiting motorcyclists because all the hotels and campsites were full. American Motorcycling Magazine said: "Daytona was the centre of American Motorcycling, and the flag-bedecked streets were packed with motorcycles bearing licence plates from every state and province."

The following year saw a longer course with more sweeping turns, although the track still combined road and beach. But the town was growing, spreading along the beach as well as outwards, and beach racing ended in 1960, the race being won by Brad Andres riding a Harley-Davidson.

A purpose-built stadium, that still hosts the main races today, was first used in 1961, and the constant need to change the date to suit the tide also ended.

Harley again took the chequered flag with Roger Reiman, whose name was to become synonymous with the marque. But times were changing, and the American bikes were to achieve only five further wins before the Japanese took over.

Over the years the track has changed in configuration and length, but the Daytona 200 has remained the central race in Cycle Week. The actual racing, however, has become less important to many of those who flock to the resort in early March, which perhaps is a good job. Despite the stadium facility covering 450 acres, it would struggle to accommodate the half a million who arrive in Daytona.

Although there is a smattering of Japanese and European bikes in attendance, one marque stands out – Harley-Davidson. Daytona is a meeting place for people from all walks of life, united by their interest in a bike that has become synonymous with America. A bike that has eschewed a lifestyle and a breed of people – Harley People!

1 *Main Street*

Daytona is split by an intercoastal waterway, leaving a narrow strip of land between it and the Atlantic Ocean. It is on this narrow tract of land that the main biking activities take place for those who are there for the festival of biking rather than the racing.

Main Street is central to the part of town located closest to the beach. It runs in a straight line from the pier before crossing over the waterway. The whole focus of attention is placed here as bikes parade up and down, to the delight of the onlooker.

The shops are full of biking memorabilia. It seems like the world's cotton crop has been used to produce souvenir T-shirts, while leathers, hats, mugs, knives, lighters – in fact anything you can think of – has the Harley logo attached.

From the first Saturday, Main Street is packed solid with people and bikes. It remains in this state until the final Sunday. Bikes are tightly parked down both sides of the street, and they are often covered in accessories costing more than the original bike!

The street is a constant parade of machines and people, from the sublime to the ridiculous, the ordinary to the bizarre. From early in the morning until the small hours – Main Street lives!

Small groups of bikes can be seen in any street in Daytona just riding around

Restful contemplation of the meaning of life and Harleys. Age is no barrier

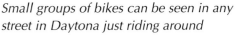

Spiders' web outfits are sexless, although they suit some better than others, and provide entertainment for on-lookers

Almost the same but not quite. Very few bikes or riders are identical in appearance

They start 'em young in the ways of Harley. Tank-top rides show the joys of motorcycling and posing down Main Street

Risking all to bare not quite all. A case of naughty but nice!

Even the buildings support the Harleys with local artists brightening up the brickwork

Patriotic, although the bike comes from down south. The warmer weather allows a different form of bike attire than one worn at home

Three wheels on a colour co-ordinated wagon, with large wardrobe space at the rear

*As time passes by you have
seen most things, but it is still
worth a look*

*In Daytona the streets
are paved with Harleys*

*A large number of the
bikes arrive by truck
owing to the distances
that have to be covered*

Just enjoying cruisin'
in the Florida sun

"Excuse me officer,
which way to the fire?"

Harley people come
from all over the
world, united by
their love of bikes

A dashing white horse is still an
eye-catcher, even if it is mechanical

An unusual gap in the normally constant stream of bikes

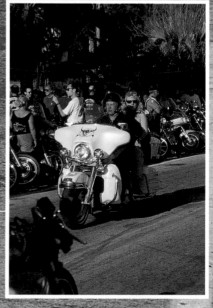

Hidden behind fairing and rider, a helmet-less pillion enjoys the view

Riding for God is as important as riding a Harley to some people

Customising the helmet to match the bike can be important

An even-tempered police rider enjoys a chat while stuck in a normal Main Street traffic queue

A typical view down Main Street

Painted bodies are as important as the artwork on a bike to some aficionados

Patches on jackets give an indication of the distance travelled to attend "Cycle Week"

Open-face crash helmets allow a few of life's other pleasures to be enjoyed as you ride along

"Hands up," and the police are nowhere in sight. Riding positions seem to be altered as much as colour schemes

"Wish we had a Harley to ride instead of the Kawasakis"

Two or three wheels – as long as it is a Harley, who cares!

If you have to leave the beach, you might as well try and keep up the sun tan and show off the tattoos!

Bird's eye view of the parade

Laid-back approach allows pillion to warn of police presence to the rear

Dark riding glasses are very much part of the scene

Shades of Peter Fonda and Easy Rider

Cheeky view of black lace riding apparel!

Age is not a problem in Main Street – all are welcome

Turn the other cheek. All forms of dress are acceptable in main street

The chance to appear on the cover of a magazine is an opportunity not to be missed

As the afternoon shadows fall, there is a slight let-up in the amount of riding

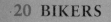

As night falls the party just keeps on going

Good vantage points are at a premium

Daytona Beach welcomes bikers and, more importantly, their money!

Laddered clothing is all the rage. A case of more for less, considering the price of it

Leather and studs is a popular form of dress for Harley people

*"I'll just put my feet up and
enjoy the free show"*

*Plenty of choice on the
clothing front in the Main
Street shops*

*Biker Art
giving a
re-enforcement
to the lifestyle*

Three wheels make roundabouts difficult to negotiate

Night falls, and the party is in full swing

2 On the Beach

Although racing no longer takes place on the white sandy beaches, they are open to traffic. Toll booths at various access points ensure that they are not over-used, and beach police keep speeds at acceptable levels.

The hard-packed area closest to the Atlantic Ocean becomes a two-way street, while the softer sand becomes a car park. Spectators pack the piers and sea front to watch the constant stream of vehicles. Those fortunate enough to be staying in the hotels that line the front can watch from their balconies, enjoying a grandstand view of the proceedings.

Although sand and salt are not compatible with motorcycle paintwork and chrome, this does not stop riders from joining in the beach parade. Despite the police patrols, crash helmets get left behind as riders and passengers enjoy the sea breeze blowing through their hair.

Most riders are only too aware that too much throttle can have the bike sideways and then on the ground in a heap. This may please the spectators but will not help maintain the bike's pristine appearance. This fact more than the speed limit signs keeps things at walking pace.

Many of the various Custom shows that take place during the week are held adjacent to the beach, allowing spectators and entrants the chance to combine biking with sun, sea and sand. The beach is still very much part of Cycle Week!

Riders parked behind cars on the firmer sand

The best of both worlds, somewhere to stay and sleep, and a bike to ride

The beach to yourself or..

..shared with others

Why wear a helmet when you can enjoy the wind in your hair?

Occasionally, even the beach comes to a halt because of the volume of traffic

Racing the tide, just like they used to

With the pier behind you, it's just open sand in front of you

Even full-dress tourers can ride on the firm sand – weight is not a problem

Arlen Ness-inspired creation enjoys the freedom of Daytona Beach

Despite a speed limit, very few adhere to it. More a case of going with the flow – or tide, if you prefer

Just cruising the beach, either alone or with company, has got to be done at least once during your stay at Daytona

Custom shows are situated close to the beach so that everyone can enjoy the best of all worlds

Custom leather artwork to match the bike at a beach custom show

Love me, love my bike!

3 Other Activities

Although many riders never leave the city limits, content to cruise around town, there is plenty on offer for those who wish to go further afield or sample the latest machinery.

The Harley factory brings large trucks full of bikes and clothing, and takes over the Ocean Centre just along from Main Street, opposite the beach.

In the vast auditorium the very latest bikes are displayed along with those of historical interest. Factory clothing is very much part of the image, and all the latest designs and styles are displayed for sale while the Harley Owners Group hosts various seminars.

A few miles up the road on the side of the race track, bikes are available for test rides along a set route. Japanese importers offer the same service, but the Harley queue is always the longest!

On the outskirts of town 'Swapmeets' cater for those looking for cheap second-hand parts and accessories, or for just a good browse, and there are various shows and competitions for the many customised bikes.

America's only 'Wall of Death' performs at the largest event in neighbouring Volusia County. It is run by descendants of the original riders on the same Harley bikes used by their grandfathers.

Some venues hold coleslaw wrestling, tattoo contests and Japanese bike bashing. Harley people come from all walks of life and have very varied interests!

The actual bike owned by a famous Harley person, singer Elvis Presley

Harley sign at the Ocean Centre

Harley-branded clothing for the real enthusiast with plenty of money

*Harley staff
discuss how
sales are going*

*Historic Harley racing machine from the
days of 'proper' beach racing*

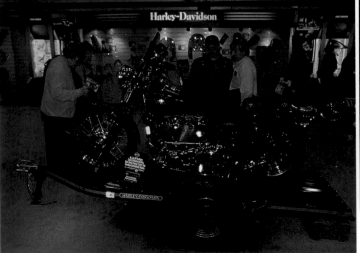

*New bikes on display for potential customers to
view at the Ocean centre*

Small Harley person aged 10 tries out
Harley Pin Ball machine for size

Most of the police bikes used by Daytona's finest are
Harleys, despite a few Kawasakis creeping in

Harley people who drive trucks
transporting road-test bikes across
the states for all to try out

One of "Charlies' Angels," who has her own Harley to fly on

Early Harley racing machine offered for sale at Swapmeet. Bargains like this are rare as the stalls tend to concentrate on later bikes

Every conceivable accessory can be bought from a stall somewhere at Daytona

Some just have to wait patiently to see what their partner has bought!

Not your usual sort of riding or shopping gear, or for that matter golfing, either!

There is no point in leaving the pets out; Harley ownership is a family affair

If you break down or have a problem, then there are plenty on hand to solve it and enable you to ride home

"You will have to know how an engine works son, so you had better start learning what's inside one now "

There are hundreds of new and used parts on offer as well as many used machines at bargain prices for those willing to rummage through boxes and haggle on prices

America's only Wall of Death still uses Harleys, built at the same time as the wall and run by descendants of the wall's founder

People will queue all day to get a ride on the latest offering from the Milwaukee factory ...

...even the police turn up for a ride if they can jump the queue

The Buell is the sports version of the Harley, and is attracting a new breed of Harley person

All in blue because they are Buell people – and ex-police!

Specials attract a lot of attention

4 *Racing*

Racing was the reason that Cycle Week started and for many is still the reason for going to Daytona. Harley may not dominate any more, but they still have a presence, especially now the very latest VR 1000 race bike is competitive with the world's best.

At the beginning of race week are two Vintage race days, and among the many old machines that do battle on the banked track are early Harley-Davidsons. Some used to compete on the beach course and are not best suited to tarmac racing, but this does not stop them being ridden hard and fast.

Towards the end of the week the Dirt Track racing takes place in the evenings at the nearby Municipal Stadium. This type of racing is still very much the preserve of Harley, although the bikes are not the traditional V-twin machines but single cylinder bikes that are broadsided at high speed.

Here, under the floodlights, Harley-Davidson is still number one!

Back at the main stadium the week's racing ends with the 200-mile event. However, in recent years the closest racing has been seen in the Harley 883 races. These are Harley 'Sportsters' that are basically road bikes with a few safety modifications for the track.

Thanks to tight policing of the rules, winning is a case of riding well rather than having large sums of money available. Many Harley dealers support riders or enter their own bikes in a series that has captured the race fans' imagination.

The new VR1000 has given them something else to root for in the main race. At present the bike is not a winner, but it will not be long before Harley recaptures the golden years of the fifties, when the marque dominated the 200-mile beach race.

Early Harleys take to the track during the two Vintage race days. Many of these hand change machines were around when the track was still part beach and part road

The Municipal Stadium hosts Dirt Track racing where Harley still reigns supreme with single cylinders rather than V-twins

Chris Carr is one of the best of the Dirt Track Harleymen, though he also mixes it on the tarmac circuits as well

Scott Parker, holder of the No 1 plate and well-known Harley devotee, rides on the loose surfaces

George Roeder, an ex-Harley works rider and still a keen fan of the Dirt track races

The legendary Harley rider of all disciplines, Jay "Springer" Springsteen

Harley fans even when spectating

The Hooters chain of restaurants are a haunt of many a Harley rider thanks to the scanty outfits of their staff (even if they do back a Japanese bike in racing)

Before the racing a huge amount of workshop preparation takes place by many unsung heroes, who ensure their riders have the best tool for the job

The Harley factory's return to racing has ensured that many personnel assist at the track to make sure all goes well with the race bike

The Harley 883 race has produced some of the closest and most interesting racing for a long time, and provides an excellent race for the spectators

It is not just a question of being there and being part of the team, you must dress correctly as well!

Close racing is guaranteed by the rules in the 883 Harley races

Shawn Higbee, holder of the No 1 plate for the 883 Harley class in America, cranks his bike through the infield turns at Daytona's banked track

Scott Zampach on his way to winning the last race at 1995 Daytona on his Harley 883

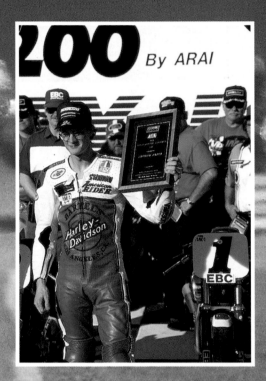

Higbee holds his second place
trophy after a close dice with
eventual winner Scott Zampach

The first three home in the 883 race,
standing in the winners' enclosure,
enjoy the spoils of victory

General racing shots of the 883 race

5 The Final Parade

Although the Daytona 200-mile race signals the end of the racing festival on the Sunday afternoon, for many their week ends in the morning with the final parade.

Bikes begin to assemble in the early hours of the morning to grab a leading position in the run. It starts by the beach and wends its way through the town before finishing at Harley Heaven, a spectator area at the side of the race track.

It is impossible to estimate the number of bikes that take part; some solo, others with passengers, but all in convoy traditionally led by the local police chief on his own bike, and often with well-known personalities in tow.

Traditionally the bikes are blessed during a short religious service, either at the start or somewhere *en route*. The end of the run signals the start of a long journey home for many, while others stay to watch the racing or just talk bikes.

Depending on the numbers taking part the convoy can take over an hour to pass any one point. The spectator is rewarded with every model and capacity of Harley spanning the decades since the firm started. Any other marques are almost unrecognisable in the heavy metal parade.

Apart from the racing, Harley-Davidson has made Daytona very much its own. The bikes and the people swamp the town and take it over for a week-long biking party hosted by Harley people!

The final parade on the Sunday morning, as thousands of riders parade through Daytona escorted by police and split only by traffic lights into smaller groups

They come in all shapes, sizes and colours, but all with Harley on the tank and all proud to be part of probably the largest convoy of motorcycles in the world

*For some, national pride is all part of the
reason for riding Harley-Davidson*

The police are there purely for the ride. On their own Harleys they are very much part of the parade

Some stand up to get a better view of the other bikes and the spectators

*You've just got to acknowledge
your adoring public!*

Many take their belongings with them ready to head home after the parade has finished.

Some take the kitchen sink home as well!

For some, the bikes go home the way they arrived – on trailers

Three wheels or two, as long as they roll under
Harley power all are welcome to join in

Time to take a chance without a crash helmet as the police are all tied up!

Time to reflect on life in general, the parade and Cycle Week

Some may be members of a group, but virtually all present are Harley people in one form or another!

"I am not sure that I believe what I am seeing!"

Bare-faced cheek!